Daniel Zberg

International Air Transportation

How airline and airport capability impacts tourism and international business

GRIN Verlag

Bibliografische Information der Deutschen Nationalbibliothek:

Die Deutsche Bibliothek verzeichnet diese Publikation in der Deutschen National-bibliografie; detaillierte bibliografische Daten sind im Internet über http://dnb.d-nb.de/ abrufbar.

Imprint:

Copyright © 2012 GRIN Verlag GmbH
Druck und Bindung: Books on Demand GmbH, Norderstedt Germany
ISBN: 978-3-656-58394-3

This book at GRIN:

http://www.grin.com/en/e-book/267126/international-air-transportation

GRIN - Your knowledge has value

Der GRIN Verlag publiziert seit 1998 wissenschaftliche Arbeiten von Studenten, Hochschullehrern und anderen Akademikern als eBook und gedrucktes Buch. Die Verlagswebsite www.grin.com ist die ideale Plattform zur Veröffentlichung von Hausarbeiten, Abschlussarbeiten, wissenschaftlichen Aufsätzen, Dissertationen und Fachbüchern.

Visit us on the internet:

http://www.grin.com/

http://www.facebook.com/grincom

http://www.twitter.com/grin_com

International Air Transportation

Week # 8 – Research Paper / TLMT342

Daniel Z'berg

28 September 2012

International Air Transportation

Air transportation is a key factor in long-term economic development, growth, and overall success. Like other forms of transportation, air travel simply provides a link between two or more different locations; though, air travel separates itself by offering a very quick alternative to travel vast distances. The unique nature of air transport has proved its significance in developed nations and the increased connectivity has recently demonstrated an even greater impact for developing economies. There are, however, substantial challenges in producing respectable air transport infrastructure in developing nations. In fact, there are also many difficulties involving air travel that affect developed nations as well. Infrastructure, costs, regulation, and sustainability are some of the more noteworthy concerns of international air transportation. Understanding the problem is the first step to creating a solution and, with tangible collaborative efforts, more efficient air transportation networks can begin to benefit the international community.

Many people likely suspect air travel as mostly serving tourists and international business professionals – and their suspicions are based on real figures. In 2005, 40% of all international tourists traveled by air – contributing to the nearly two billion passengers who travel by air each year (ATAG, 2005). In addition to leisure travel, providing access to virtually anywhere facilitates international trade and can benefit all economies involved. For example, a pineapple company based in Hawaii might not have any more arable land to expand their plantation. The company could look to foreign direct investment to purchase land in another country such as the Philippines. If the Hawaiian business people have no quick access to the Philippines, trading would not be feasible. The Hawaiian company can fly to the Philippines to purchase the land, coordinate logistics operations, and complete the transaction. Travelling by a water carrier might be possible, but the time it would take to complete a journey would deter businesses from trading. It is no wonder the Air Transport Action Group cites 70% of businesses report "serving a bigger market is a key benefit of using air services" (ATAG, 2005). It is apparent that providing access and connectivity is the foundation of the economic benefits offered by air transportation.

In addition to connectivity, air transport allows certain items to support remote operations that can benefit a developing nation with little other transportation infrastructure. For instance, there is high demand in developed nations for raw materials found in Africa. Gold and uranium mining in the landlocked states of Mali and Niger account for over seventy percent of their gross national income respectively (Bastke, 2008). The mines are in remote locations in the countries and aviation is used extensively to bring perishable supplies and fly the resources to larger hubs (Bastke, 2008). Like the African mines, other developing nations could benefit from receiving support through air transport. Workers in remote locations might depend on aircraft to bring fresh fruits and vegetables and important medical supplies.

The delivery of medical and other perishable supplies can serve an indirect economic purpose by supporting remote trading operations; furthermore, similar shipments can create social benefits in developing regions as well. The speedy nature of air transport allows social benefits by delivering medical supplies, emergency relief, and humanitarian aid. Additionally, having more variety can improve the quality of life for citizens in developing nations.

Developing economies are aware of the potential and significant air transportation growth is transpiring around the world. Passenger air travel grew 8.9% in the Middle East and 10.2% in Latin America in 2011 (Raytheon, 2012), adding to a global growth trend that boasted over 45% between 1980 and 2005 (ATAG, 2005). Deregulation is a major reason for the massive growth in the industry. Allowing airlines to compete in the free market is commonly considered a major impetus for the airline industry to increase efficiency and lower prices, thus facilitating an increase in passengers. The reduction of price is a direct result of deregulation. After adjusting for inflation, the cheapest round-trip New York-Los Angeles flight that the government would allow was $1,442 in 1974 ("Airline deregulation", 2011). The same route – again, adjusted for inflation – could cost as little as $268 ("Airline deregulation", 2011). Such a disparity in ticket costs is a clear reason for an increase in passenger travel.

Despite the apparent successes of deregulation, many officials around the world are reluctant to hand over their airline industry to the private sector. The sentiment is particularly present in developing nations, where corruption in politics is often a major problem. Air transportation in the least developed nations is at risk even with government regulation. Many of the world's least developed nations have authoritarian governments that are at constant risk of strikes, coups, impermeable bureaucracy, and high crime rates (Bastke, 2008). The self-serving nature of totalitarian regimes creates a barrier for those wanting to privatize the industry to allow for growth and better service.

The World Bank is the central organization leading the effort toward the privatization of air transportation around the world (Hussain, 2008). The motives of The World Bank, however, are questionable. The World Bank could make a large sum of money off of the interest gained from loaning capital to businesses in developing nations. There is an inherent flaw in the argument to deregulate the industry in developing nations – there is already significant growth and creating even higher growth rates might not be sustainable. For example, India boasted 24% growth in 2004 and Indian airlines reported ordering 750 new aircraft in the same year (Hussain, 2008). Such ambition to grow seems to be having a positive impact on the economy in India; however, their safety record is severely blemished from oversights as a direct result of the rapid growth. In 2010, India announced its goal of building 315 new airports by 2020 – and domestic airlines would require 3,000 more aircraft as a result (Singh, 2010). A byproduct of the rapid expansion is accomplishing the bare minimum safety requirements. In the city of Bajpe, a runway did not meet the internationally recommended safety requirements. For example, its runway had a 295-foot overrun instead of the internationally recommended 787 feet and air traffic control did not have the benefit of a precision radar system (Singh, 2010). The result of these safety shortcomings resulted in the crash of an Air India Express flight that killed 159 people (Singh, 2010). In this instance, it is apparent that deregulation is having a negative impact on aviation safety in India.

One of the ways to help ensure India and other developing nations have the capital they need to safely expand their privatized airline industry is to remove trade barriers. Not only do trade barriers allow for other nations to benefit from the increased trade possibilities, but it also allows for foreign investors to benefit from the growing industry. Allowing more foreign investment in the airlines would mean the government could focus more on the infrastructure. For example, a foreign investor could provide the capital to start an airline in India. Without a stable infrastructure, however, there will not be enough confidence in the market to generate substantial foreign direct investment. The Federal Aviation Administration understands the benefits of improving infrastructure in other countries and has signed agreements to promote aviation safety in a number of countries "including China, India, Mexico and Brazil, as well as the European Union and the Latin American Civil Aviation Commission" (ICAO, 2011, p.32). A developing nation that creates a solid infrastructure can remove trade barriers as a way to safely generate massive amounts of economic growth.

Even though deregulation has exhibited general success in industrialized countries, there are some issues that could be cause for concern for developing nations. Nearly all of the major airlines in the United States have filed for bankruptcy including United, Delta, US Airways, Northwest, and Continental ("History", 2011). Such a failure in a lesser-developed nation could seriously impact the economy, as the government might have problems supporting bailouts for their flagship carriers.

Another issue plaguing airlines is simply balancing supply and demand. Simchi-Levy, et. al. (2008) note a significant Boeing Aircraft write-down of $2.6 billion in 1997 due to "raw material shortages, internal and supplier parts shortages and productivity inefficiencies" (p.5). Failures in demand management result in poor forecasting and can lead to significant losses. All economies that depend on stable air transport are affected by such a loss; however, developing nations would be more severely impacted as the industry seeks to play a more significant role in its economic growth.

To mitigate risk, airlines are not fully deregulated. There are a number of authorities that airlines must answer to, mostly in order to ensure the safety of the public. According to Coyle, et. al. (2008), regulation in the United States is growing in some areas and "legislation has been passed to improve the safety of the transportation industry, reduce its impact on the environment, and defend the country against terrorism" (p.406). The new rules have resulted in higher prices for passengers in the United States and contributed to major bankruptcies. If international authorities follow suit, developing nations will be forced to follow the strict new rules as well – possibly hindering growth.

European Union regulations include a blacklist of foreign carriers. Under direction of the European Commission, there are over 100 airlines that are blacklisted or severely restricted from operating in the European Union ("Air safety", 2012). All aircraft based in the Philippines, including their major flagship carrier, are prohibited from operating in the EU ("Air safety", 2012). The impact of such legislation can be devastating for the airlines and tourism of the Philippines. The ban on the airlines can cast doubt on the entire industry. Wilfred Manue, associate professor at the Asian Institute of Management, states that "if a country's civil aviation authority appears not to be implementing what the ICAO requires . . . the validity of the certifications issued by the civil aviation authority to airlines is now in doubt" (Grace, 2010).

It would seem that tourism would not be drastically affected because there are a number of international carriers that meet higher safety standards; however, travelling by aircraft outside the major hub introduces a unique problem. According to Ace Durano, the Tourism Secretary, European insurance companies "have stopped covering travelers for domestic air travel in the country, leading to the cancellation of bookings for April to August to the Philippines by travel operators from Germany, the United Kingdom and France" (Grace, 2010). This correlates with National Statistics Coordination Board data claiming that Europeans made up 10% of foreign tourists in Philippines in 2008 (Grace,

2010). For the Philippines, it is clear they must invest in their air infrastructure to improve their international ratings – otherwise the nation cannot realize the full benefits of air transportation.

The domino effect caused by a poor international safety rating can strike a severe blow to a nation's aviation. Another concern for air transportation in both industrialized nations and the developing world is security. In the U.S., the Transportation Security Administration (TSA) is responsible for safety of flight on both freighter and passenger aircraft. In an effort to thwart terrorism, the TSA and Customs & Border Patrol have created rules and regulations that make it more difficult for passengers to fly, mail things internationally, and enter the U.S. in general. Policymakers have also designed agreements with some partners to build confidence in the security programs maintained by other international trading companies (David & Stewart, 2010). The Customs-Trade Partnership Against Terrorism (C-TPAT) is a partnership program that gives an incentive to cargo shipped by participating countries (David & Stewart, 2010). By encouraging companies to boost their own security, the burden on the government is lessened and less spending is required; however, the total cost of ownership will go up due to the fixed costs associated with providing security. In the end, it is a small price to pay to reduce the threat of terrorism.

Developing nations may not agree. In lesser-developed countries with high trade barriers, initial capital for infrastructure improvements like security are sometimes viewed a luxury, not a necessity. Some airports might not have metal detectors, x-ray machines, secure terminals or passenger holding areas. With the threat of terrorism in the forefront of the minds in developed nations, developing nations will be forced to invest in proper security improvements. Removing trade barriers to allow for more foreign direct investment might help to eliminate some of the weight involved in improving the overall security of air transport in a nation.

In summary, the benefits of air transportation are substantial – particularly for developing nations. Long-term economic growth is facilitated by the connectivity provided by air travel's ability to travel long distances in a short amount of time. Unfortunately, generating the capital to boost air transport infrastructure can be difficult for developing nations that simply do not have the economic means to provide state of the art aircraft and equipment. Safety issues continue to be addressed in some developing nations and problems have resulted in downgrades that have proven harmful to the economies involved. Safety issues appear to be the result of the aviation industry growing faster than the economies can support. One way to solve many of the problems associated with international air transport infrastructure is to remove trade barriers to create opportunities for foreign direct investment. Allowing more foreign direct investment in domestic air travel will allow developing economies to focus on the safety and security at airports; thus, growth in the industry would be properly supported by a solid infrastructure.

References

Air safety. (2012). European Commission. Retrieved from

http://ec.europa.eu/transport/air-ban/list_en.htm

Airline deregulation, revisited. (2011). *BusinessWeek.* Retrieved from

http://www.businessweek.com/stories/2011-01-20/airline-deregulation-

revisitedbusinessweek-business-news-stock-market-and-financial-advice

ATAG. (2005). The economic & social benefits of air transport. Air Transport Action

Group. Retrieved from

http://www.icao.int/Meetings/wrdss2011/Documents/JointWorkshop2005/ATAG

_SocialBenefitsAirTransport.pdf

Bastke, P. (2008). Assisting air transport in developing nations. City University; London.

Retrieved from http://www.gapan.org/ruth-documents/study-

papers/Bastke%20Peter.pdf

Coyle, J., Langley, C., Gibson, B., Novack, R., and Bardi, E., (2009). *Supply chain*

management; A logistics perspective. Ohio: South-Western Press. 8th Ed.

David, P., & Stewart, R.. (2010). *International logistics.* 3rd Ed. Mason, OH:

Thomson ISBN 13: 978-1-111-21955-0

Grace, J. (2010). EU ban darkens Philippine skies. *Asia Times.* Retrieved from

http://www.atimes.com/atimes/Southeast_Asia/LD20Ae01.html

Hussain, M. Z. (2010). Investment in Air Transport Infrastructure. Retrieved from

http://www.ppiaf.org/sites/ppiaf.org/files/publication/Investment_Air_Transport_

MZHussain.pdf

ICAO. (2011). State of global aviation safety. International Civil Aviation Organization.

Retrieved from http://www.icao.int/safety/Documents/ICAO_State-of-Global-
Safety_web_EN.pdf

Raytheon. (2012). Air traffic needs an upgrade as developing countries become more
affluent, fly more: Expert. Retrieved from
http://www.raytheon.com/media/fia12/atm/

History of U.S. airline bankruptcies. (2011). *FoxBusiness.com.* Retrieved from
http://www.foxbusiness.com/travel/2011/11/29/history-us-airline-bankruptcies/

Simchi-Levi, D., Kaminsky, P., Simchi-Levi, E. (2008). *Designing and managing the
supply chain: Concepts, strategies and case studies,* 3rd ed. New York, NY:
McGraw Hill.

Singh, M. (2010). Has the rush to grow made Indian air travel unsafe? *Time.* Retrieved
From http://www.time.com/time/world/article/0,8599,1992800,00.html

Lightning Source UK Ltd.
Milton Keynes UK
233998UK00004B/17